There Will Be Singing

Aidan Semmens

There Will Be Singing

Shearsman Books

First published in the United Kingdom in 2020 by
Shearsman Books Ltd
PO Box 4239
Swindon
SN3 9FN

Shearsman Books Ltd Registered Office
30–31 St. James Place, Mangotsfield, Bristol BS16 9JB
(this address not for correspondence)

www.shearsman.com

ISBN 978-1-84861-720-9

ACKNOWLEDGMENTS
Thanks to Maria Stadnicka and Kelvin Corcoran
for support and advice

and to the editors of the following magazines, in which many of these poems
have appeared, in some cases in earlier versions or excerpts:

*Blackbox Manifold, Free Verse, Golden Handcuffs Review, International Times,
Jacket, Litmus, Long Poem Magazine, Noon, Perfect Bound, Shearsman,
Smithereens, Stride, Tears in the Fence, Tentacular,* and
The 2013 Salt Anthology of New Writing

Contents

Wonders of the Age

Wonders of the Age	13
Dancers and Architects	16
The People's Welfare Typewriter	18
In a Holy Place	19
Light Falls	21
Work Made Free	23
Palimpsest I	25
By a Wayside Shrine	27

The People's Palace of Dream

Jahangir and the Hoopoe	31
Lines in the Sand	32
Haematite	33
Red	34
For His Bad Verses	35
Palimpsest II	36
Armistice Day	37
And Afterwards?	41
Goodbye Don't Mean I'm Gone	42

A Clergyman's Guide to String Theory

Googled Earth	45
Talking Out of School	47
Thirty-four Statements Amounting to a Definition	48
A Clergyman's Guide to String Theory	50
Ark of Marvels	57
Museum Piece	59
If You Live Long Enough You See Everything	60

Halifax Road

Lunchtime May 27th   63
Domes of Silence   64
Halifax Road   65
Phyllis   67
Palimpsest III   69
Three Vignettes for Tom Raworth   71
Day Trip 1978   73
That Strange Geometry   75
Saddleworth   79
Forbidden Morning   80

In memory of Hilary Semmens, née Rainbow, 1921-2016

and for Maria Stadnicka

In den finsteren Zeiten
Wird da auch gesungen werden?
Da wird auch gesungen werden.
Von den finsteren Zeiten.
    —*Bertolt Brecht*

Wonders of the Age

Wonders of the Age

anticipate what you will this edifice
will not disappoint you
certain localities like certain people
please us at first sight

at once you are transported
back to the days of the patriarchs
throngs of elegant vehicles pass
and repass every afternoon

you are a nomad, a voyager
on a petrified ocean
with rolling waves of sand
close by a ruined fountain

at which combatants would wash
after the conflict, petted and admired
by soft white hands
patting brawny musculature

some vegetation covers
this apparently barren rock
and frequently the mouth of a cannon
protrudes from a bed of flowers

to a certain extent all seaside places
resemble one another
the pleasureseekers depart
with the first cold autumnal storm

they nevertheless preserve unchanged
their forefathers' primitive habits of dress
their costumes exceedingly odd and amusing
their lives toilsome and cheerless

lined with quaint and picturesque
mediaeval buildings and that fatal field
where the modern mingles
with ancient gaiety, splendour and woe

before the rude cabins
rise frequently tall foul posts
carved from top to bottom
into grotesque resemblances

with their unintelligible decorations
letterings and mysterious rooms
the combination of monosyllables
slip from the memory like drops of water

the entire audience smokes
and the performance goes on amid hideous
beating of drums and gongs
the gambling dens and opium cellars

should be visited in company
of a policeman and pilgrim troops
in tenement houses of men dozing
in half-drugged sleep

in this paradise inhabited by devils
it is clatteringly difficult to imagine
how a photographer ever contrived
to represent the street as tranquil

for civilisation is immeasurably
to be preferred to despotism
and here the hallowed waters are lined
with temples and booths where idols are sold

the science of the ascent has now
been reduced to a system –
with fine weather and suitable precaution
there is no very serious danger

grip the thread or wire well
between your thumb and middle finger
and pull gently but firmly
until the mechanism releases

do not attempt to imagine
what consequences your action may have

Dancers and Architects

on warm windless nights
the old termite mounds sparkle
with eerie green light
flashed by click-beetle larvae
living in the outer layers

you may be struck by the contrast
between the leaf's cool blue
and the glow of the fire
seeping through the wound

shifting winds make flames of the dancing sand
lightning lacerates the sky, lava lighting
the swelling smoke
a breeze pushes the animals along
like tiny boats

elegant swimmers, they will glide
right into you, gently nudging
you out of their way, she says

waterlilies stretch up to sunlight
through a green layer of mist
in a once sacred sinkhole

low cloud covers the meadow
and apollos shelter among the grasses

the male pauses
in his pre-dawn display
tail and wings fanned and fluffed
against the backdrop of the forest
then turns his back on her
brushes her face with his wire plumes

the massive gorgonian coral shelters
by day a shoal of tiny cardinal fish

a geological event, extreme heat deep
within the continental crust
gave rise to the crystal formation

an almond tree where fireflies gather
patterns of light moving constantly
on the surface of a forest pool

planktonic animals nightdiving in deep water
contrasts in movement and texture
patterned fish sheltering among swaying tentacles

tangled silvery threads, the rivers
and deltas change from day to day
a firework display in slow motion
a giant puffball frantic with activity

tendrils coiled like clefs
on a musical stave

The People's Welfare Typewriter

calls upon you to
imagine Sisyphus happy
imagine tulips
codfish
coffee
imagine the fervour
of the early typists

"thoughts travel the roads
that writing makes"
or so they say

it's said that language limits thought
words and signs unreadable
in an incompatible country

begin then by studying railways
or the keys that shine with use:
emigrant
far away
urgent
longing
hardship
dream

typists more than anyone
must follow the times

In a Holy Place

the ruin is uninhabited
except by a seemingly ancient
wooden statue of the virgin

odd visions of maybe familiar
people on an unfamiliar street
an altar to the unknown goddess

illustrations of bewildering plants
charts of impossible heavens
female figures in a heavy hand

their postures and activities
having no parallel
in words or their erasure

the agents of conformity
pound highway and byway, not all
their weaponry metaphorical

in this brick structure great families
holy men and mystics meet
women with the saintliest of looks

Brueghel and Dürer study alchemy and law
clocks and musical instruments
in neat but unreadable glyphs

penned into tight cryptographic circles
the manuscript sold at a humiliating price
now available online, alien

fighter pilots and tank commanders
need to focus quickly
on all this corrugated dereliction

coming from an urban neighbourhood
places you in a higher category of risk
where it's not wealth that counts, but change

no one ever launched a war for numbers
and logic won't do it
we need a story, a moral decocted

from the most limited evidence
simple words in a half-formed language
sinister analysis of ritual codes

or perhaps, satirically, vice versa
musicians and enthusiasts, ghosts
at the soft edges of consciousness

mission creep and collateral damage
sipped from exotic, esoteric glasses
in bunkers that may not be secure

beneath their breath, hands holding
red and black cards, the ace of wands
gently waving in a breeze

Light Falls

not yet halfway to the summit
we pause to take in the view –
on a stretch of road near the power plant
abandoned vehicles swallowed
by trees and grass, a chained-up motorbike
absorbed into the land

above perhaps raptors or ravens
and a stray gleam
of something you can't make out
or tiny icicles of breath
caught in the shining air

dust of the country, dust of the town
weave together on the wind

where a traveller might stumble
on an ancient site
old men sit under arches, tombs
robbed of artefact and bone

places have voices not their own
yet I am snatched back
to a land of lawns, sunset malls
coldest recorded winters
the room dark and a man
writing, moving his hands

the lost game of self
and making it all up
we watched the news
with the sound turned down
on secular transcendence
of falling towers, tear-streaked

infants in bombed-out plazas
migrants at the gates
of a gated hell
crusts in their multilingual hands
at the alarm-wired portal
the revelations of February
triumphs of industry and agriculture
a glimpse behind the scenes at the congress
splendid acts of desecration

you say nothing we remember today
may be of significance tomorrow
to see is not to understand
things photographed or passed over
old texts that speak of mysteries
the sick asleep in temple sanctuaries
for fear of the image
reification of the word

a pale sky scratched by contrails
erasures in the view
misleading shadows
uninterpretable space
impressions of movement and gradations
of light travelling obliquely
casting reflections glistening
on sea or city streets

and how we learn what happened here
in passing fragments, not quite believing
or not wanting to believe

Work Made Free

We eat lunch in a restaurant
close to the industrial area,
menu and prices aimed carefully
at a new managerial class;

videos of a funeral cortège
repeat endlessly behind the diners' heads
in a porcelain-white environment
of cutlery and chairs.

The queen in this story is a malnourished child,
the same fly permanently buzzing
about her lip sores and tarnished tiara;

there is a chicken loose in the chocolate factory,
entrails spilling from its ravaged arse
among the cocoa solids.

They're all in special economic zones,
old refurbished buildings from a communist era,
jobs traded on the out-of-stock exchange
nodes in the global supply chain.

Factories on the flat horizon mark the land,
crumbling brickwork shedding plaster
in buildings where pot plants
tower over TV sets;

shadowy workers whose homes
remain always just out of shot
start with a live chicken
and it comes out minutes later in trays
with little skill and plastic film applied,

intruders on their own land
displaced by state-creation.
The border's not much higher
than a farmyard fence

priests on one side
penitents on the other;
theorists of borderlessness
and market regulation
say the wall is the will of the people.
From a distance *trompe-l'oeil* gaps
invite you through;

slogans above the entranceway
Work, Have Fun and Live Safely
etched in the glass
we are all
Connected Through Joy.

Palimpsest I

A play on words of Maria Stadnicka and Jessica Mookherjee

Imagine this: a carriage crossing the steppes;
you are leaning against the window
singing, watching the spiders;
barbed wire turns to light
and someone looks like you
in some workplace surrounded by boxes.
In your chest is a bird
caught by the opening
lungs knocking against frozen hours;
our approach is heading north,
the landscape accelerating,
fingers touching cold glue.
The sounds move in circles,
smaller and smaller, our eyes
as far off as birds.
From our careless enclosure
we like to see ourselves fall, knowing
the physical nature of human pain,
perfume of amber, sacks of oil
and oozing fish skins,
animal damage and a fog
of our own blood, transported
by sea. The train exists only
in our stomachs – we have no time
to make good all we have undone,
broken, boiled, muscles extracted,
fire and string by the ditch.
Our face turns north, through glass
hours spread frozen on thin cellophane ribbons,
curved mud, hand sliding easily over a map.
We shred a broken ship,
keep a wreck in style,
and all your spilled shopping –

the wafer, the wine, the whale blood,
coal and dripping fat, the damned
owls still dancing
and all the things we'll need
when the weather gets bad.
Labelled samples from the surgery,
genetic disordering,
which so seldom makes the news.
We wake in a series of assemblies,
tailing off beyond
the dipping four-wave coastline,
then commercials, green glass
sea and we are still
sleeping outside
on our common ground.

By a Wayside Shrine

How far, then, do those gods of yours protect you
from the brutalities of strangers,
the sins and things of living?

We come from Bucovina and from Pliskova,
from Stalingrad and Ur, our hammers and our hoes
beaten and shaven into musketry and halberds,

we arrive by longship, raft and frigate,
by troika and Sikorsky,
bent and bundled in the backs of vans,
in troop trains, trucks and ocean liners,

escaping factories and evading fires
that gather round the rooms
we tried to make a living in
with livid looms in martial mills.

There has never been so much
fucking in odd corners.

Angels cluster in those malodorous clouds
that linger over burned-out towers
inaptly and unsafely clad
by bureaucrats routinely on the take
because that's just how things stand.

With fingers in every pocket
the people's chosen malefactors
ease their way on shiny palms
while others can go hang.

There has never been so much
smoke hanging over the suburbs.

That place where high king Brian, Murchad
and Toirdelbach died, earl Sigurd
and Brodir of Man were slain
is become a suburban transport hub:
from here you may catch a train to Connemara
or a plane to Timbuktu – you may even
have a hovercraft to carry you home.

We come from Gondwara and the Heights of Abraham,
from caves carved under cratered cities
and plains where the buffalo formerly roamed.
We come by battlebus
with bent backs
to harvest your provender
and sweep your streets clean
of every incriminating trace.

There has never been so much
blood on the nighttime streets.

Your death may be a metaphor
and yet still be your death;
it may creep up on you unawares
or catch you smack, a swallowtail
on a windscreen.

There has never been so much
wrath in the public prints.

There has never been so much
fucking in odd corners.

The People's Palace of Dream

Jahangir and the Hoopoe

Jahangir looks at the hoopoe.

There are many hoopoes in the palace grounds
but this is the one Jahangir looks at.
Its plumage matches the russet earth of the pathway
and the flowerbed, almost blends in.
Hoopoes are ground-feeders, with bills made for probing;
perhaps they keep the ants down.

The hoopoe looks at Jahangir.

He is sedate, still, upright, clean in mostly white.
He does not look exactly like his familiar miniature
but the resemblance is close.
The hoopoe does not know this.
Perhaps it cannot distinguish Jahangir
from the bent figure sweeping the ants.

Jahangir and the hoopoe look at one another.

Is the hoopoe male or female?
Is the sweeper female or male?
Are the hoopoe and Jahangir each astonished
by the other's headdress?

Lines in the Sand

here in the People's Palace of Dream
we approve old posters of the martyrs
faded now nearly to white
on shrunken city walls that have seen
better times

applaud with nostalgia
slogans from the era of revolt
public executions for witchcraft
committed by those who signed up
for a gun and a new pair of trousers

the desert too encroaches
whispering among the living spaces
preserving ageless libraries
from our depredations
in airless dessication

spread towards us on the wind
as we edge away in our anxiety
rival militias headquartered
in the former university
and a disused zoo

this child's grin has lost its charm
along with its teeth
not from growth and replacement
but the imposition of discipline
and the handle of a spade

Haematite

ironstone, bloodstone
veins point direction
to the pole
rusty defilings
                 of old wounds
castigate abuses
                    of the tongue
its streak and powder
tawny russet
             partaking of
the doctrine of the blood

the colouring principle
of logwood
bitter to the taste
crystallising
             in laminae
of reddish-white
acid
     astringent
in which a person can see
only in artificial light

the haemerobaptist
bathes every day
to cleanse the blood
with excess of ammonia
it forms a splendid
purple matter

Red

as that brightly painted bench
quietly shining
in the early
           morning sun
of the station platform
among the wires
           the papers
and the commuter birdsong

drips on the paving
and the questions they evoke

For His Bad Verses

in every small apocalypse
on every silver screen
in low-res monochrome footage
from street-corner cameras
we see at several angles
the death of Cinna the poet

how his clothes are torn
his glasses crushed
his hair pulled
lips and ears ripped
eyes gouged genitals despoiled
limbs wrenched apart
by unmercy of the riot
hungry angry wants
both legitimate
and illegitimate
democratically unmet
turned furiously
on the innocent

how the yellow-jackets clamour
and rebel for misplaced cause
how we are gripped in a tidal swamp
of our own incontinent piss
how we elect our own demise
how nothing is as we believed
how the city and the forest burn
how the world and the worm turn

Palimpsest II

They have bought me a fragrance
from all the dead whales
found in the sleeves, upcountry flesh
and all. Taken by the tailfin, we keep
clear of the burning ship, watching
the milk sour and blacken – are you
married now? The milk
tastes of newsprint. He handles her hair
as if it were an udder.

Armistice Day

the leaves have been late to turn
hanging on for the next big storm
blackberries still on the bush in November

bemedalled gents in well-shined shoes
strut and shout around the town
playing soldiers for charity
while boys in uniform
hide in the churchyard
to set off fireworks
in lieu of guns at eleven

another boarded-up shop appears
in the award-nominated high street

four months to go
and still you don't know
where you're going

what would it? what will it?
the past devours the future

not what is the trouble
but what seems to be
what's to become of us all
in thrall to the fetish
of complex cross-border supply chains
and just-in-time delivery

a hardening of borders and arteries
a physical manifestation
promising 'the end of welfare
as we know it'

a moral responsibility to children
husbands, the church, the bank

his goodness the vice-gerent
planning the great dissolution
plots the dismantling of old institutions
and how it will enrich the elite

29 miles of leaked
local government reports
pending agreements and negotiations

on the make, currying favour while ensuring
a pile and a name for himself

visions of medicine and care
sex, family and the body

white gills of destroying angel
by the path behind the house

firms face collateral damage
new administrative burdens
market access
to developing countries
agriculture
tariffs are very high
bargaining power reduced
there are limits
to what we can do

family structures under strain
conform to norms that make things worse

structural changes to government revenue
in the global economy
access abroad and all that jazz
returned to negative growth

permanent reduction of output
changes abrupt and volatile
disruption inevitable like
the night the pound plummeted

places like Aberdeen and London
face increases
in perceived downside risk
but smaller negative effects
still difficult to adjust

avoid crossborder leakage
delays in access
to medical supplies
international markets
where agri-exports go
no safety net
for airlines
a shortage of workers
exposes local farmers

hippies and activists
are brought into line by debt
freedom to invent yourself
bought by inherited wealth

a thousand new statutory instruments
where the value of capital
rises faster than wages
trashes the meritocratic vision
dependency and care are family matters

locked in the bedroom tax of austerity
what interest must be paid
to the bank of mum and dad?

there must be a word for
experiments in faith-based welfare
effective altruism
entrepreneurship and community
as such strange alliances emerge

moral logistics become imperatives
in a place where anything may be
defined as capital
the future dividend perhaps
of a good night out with friends

in the end
whose generals
would you rather trust
if you truly had a choice?

life goes on but perhaps
it's going nowhere
in particular
nowhere to be seen
crime become
an act of charity
or charity a crime

And Afterwards?

In the town they are putting up roadblocks
widening trenches for history or power
constructing great buildings
a castle with nine towers in the high street.

Ah yes, you say, but who are these they?
What homes do they go to at the day's end
whose husbands and wives
sit down to eat with?

For whom are they blocking the roads?
Will there be beans in the shops tomorrow?
Will there be shops? Beans in packets
or tins? Voices trembling on the air.

When did you last count the roofs?
The doors, the windows, the lost
empty walls, the faceless
lurking in shadow
the cars and all the lorries
still at the roadside.

Goodbye Don't Mean I'm Gone

Nothing that happens in the roadside cabin
is his doing or his choice;

outside among the waiting men
the air is grey with condensed breath
and cheap smoke, fumes
from heavy engines slowly turning over
to retain a little warmth
and the illusion of readiness.

Few words are passed among them;
for some perhaps it matters
where the dead are buried,
on what patch of earth
the border line is drawn.

A Clergyman's Guide to String Theory

Googled Earth

A painted woman is peering through the window,
peeking from behind the aspidistra;
do not catch her impossibly radiant blue eye –
it will follow you everywhere.

Down by the harbour a man in a comical hat
is sorting fish from fish
box by box, his attention
so wrapt in scales and eyes
he seems not to notice
the wound in his thumb
from which his trickling blood
mixes with that of the catch.

A god is standing by the gateway to the underground.
Should you notice him you'd see a faraway look
in eyes that reflect a different sky.
The contortions of the mad are carved in coad stone
on pediments poised above entrances
to the house of nostalgia and guns
where previously they played;

the museum is styled imperial
for the nation's success
in exporting war to those faraway places
where spilled blood was visible only on the map:

the suicidal error of the abominated Teutons
was to attempt their genocide
so close to home.

Storm clouds conceal
whatever's left of the sun

and hope's last dictionary
dangles a well-turned phrase
but you do not understand where you are going;
nothing that's sure to work has been agreed.

The hunt for unclaimed bones goes on
beneath a helicopter sky,
a child's loot toy
fur-grimed in an untended hedge.

What takes place beneath
those acres of plain roofing
in zones where the map appears blank?
And where shall we go
if the map is wrongly drawn?
Is the shivering of the children
from excitement, fear or cold?
Is it the future we dread, or the past?

What happened, they say, is unimaginable
and you may try to console yourself
by imagining all this
is in imagination only,
that the disturbed sounds

beyond the high lattice
mean neither conflict nor threat,
that this cell and its too-familiar walls
are mere artefacts
in the wrong eye of your mind
and yourself merely a character
in one of your own fictions.

Talking Out of School

The crow now approaching the seminary roof
reveals itself as it lands as a reverend father,
wrapping its cloak around books and papers,
interfering with signals
from the wave transmitter mast.

She visits the school where Einstein studied physics,
gives an address on the great man's ethical theory,
the political power of the fuck,
later is murdered by two smartphone operatives
with nothing else to do.

There are schools of thought as there are schools of fishes
if no more than a dialectical pair
then we're surely screwed,
the roar in the night the rumble of flying engines
and nobody piloting the whale.

Thirty-four Statements
Amounting to a Definition

Unseen dangers lurk beneath the grassblades of your lawn.

A mountain cannot be trusted to remain where it is mapped.

The blackbird does not know how closely its song resembles
Mozart's 40th symphony.

At one moment the number of mobile phones equalled the number
of living alligators.

The patterns of motorway traffic may be described as a form of
Brownian motion.

The motion of bees may be discerned in shopping malls.

A man has reached adulthood without ever having a name.

There is a woman who has never been seen.

The piano was invented in Bolivia in the year 1216.

There are several species of worm that breed only in the catacombs
of Paris.

This former jihadi and publican is now an itinerant bookseller.

This cola contains several unknown substances.

Some rainbows contain more colours than others.

A mistranslated copy of the Book of Genesis has been found in a
cache of dinosaur bones.

Spinoza and Pocahontas became secret lovers in Brussels.

A mile below the Antarctic ice is a stone in the shape of St Basil's
cathedral.

This ancient petroglyph may be decoded as a periodic table of
elements.

From a certain angle, all inhabitable planets form a perfect image of
the Mona Lisa.

For certain species all perceptible existence lies within the wave-
lengths we see as green.

In the basement of my house is an incalculable number of
unexplored corridors.

The warm night conceals artworks and aardvaarks.

The bear you see in this picture is a 23-storey building.

These shoes were once worn by a Californian war-lord.

Most of the Earth's surface has been seen only by fish.

Communication has been achieved between Bratislava and
Bangkok using an old nail file and a television set.

Piltdown Man was fluent in several Polynesian languages.

In certain Sumerian dialects the number three is unpronounceable.

The most intelligent person in the world is the fifth daughter of a
subsistence farmer.

The colour vermilion is unknown in Letchworth Garden City.

Deep in the Mariana Trench lies a phonographic cylinder of Enrico
Caruso singing Dixie.

St Anthony of Padua passed messages to the KGB hidden
chemically in a phial of urine.

The relative acidity of Beethoven's concertos has never been
accurately measured.

Plato and Aristotle scratched their names on the Berlin Wall.

It is impossible to prove whether the Mona Lisa winks when
unobserved.

In some worlds this poem contains a thirty-fifth proposition.

A Clergyman's Guide to String Theory

I dropped into line with the women
rich clusters of columbine heavy and dark
there is a serene repose in the body
both sacred and sordid
surrounded by scaffolding
a face cut into stone the steps strewn with lavender
selection of articles collectible figurines and large scenes
a few pieces in relief entirely made by hand
ancient hunters and gatherers painted figures
of animals and humans in shades
of red and yellow ochre
on the cliffs that line the innumerable waterways
the stones could be seen to have been laid by hand
not thrown in randomly
and it was obvious that they were undisturbed
the Egyptians perfected the art of embalming
we no longer peer at grotesque figures
through a glass darkly
Schrödinger and Pauli meeting in dream
consider the steeple at Ulm
its unsurpassed height and the relative times
of travel taken by sound
and a falling object
for four long months
Don Juan swept through Europe
a gust of anarchy blowing
across the well-groomed parks
of church and palace
the mountains ride along a great sweep of horizon
only their snowy peaks visible
a wisp of deft strokes lightly applied
mythic and illusory as a rainbow
few tombs can be compared with this
for beauty and solemnity

by far the most important beauty treatment for the eyes
is to ensure they look upon the world with kindness
the vulgar speech soon became recognised
as a vehicle for general literature
tribes which had done little but tear and devour
one another the worshippers of a thousand
discordant falsehoods
were knit together into a nation
a megalithic tomb at Saumur
once contained a café
a Musulman chief spread his couch
at the communion table and on the altar
sacrificed each night
the virginity of a Christian nun
in smaller places the arrival
of the boat from England
was a great event
in 1620 the Pilgrim Fathers
fleeing intolerance of faith
to establish America
did so aboard a vessel named for a bloom
that reeks inescapably of sex
scholars tended to think
in terms of neatly bounded
named peoples or nations
it took about 17 days to India
black-hulled ships with high-sounding names
stoop-shouldered veterans sickly from a thousand fevers
a dissenting priest is a figure of the absurd
this visual revolution the expression of a spiritual one
the pot itself is made on a faster wheel
most houses have about 20 lighting points
but each point does not need a separate circuit
a typical recipe for a powder to throw on the fire
was one ounce each of choice storax
calamite or wood of aloes
mixed in a mortar with rose-

water of Damascus
the use of the handprint
offers the perfect symbol of the connective nature
between the rock spirit world and artist
the nova the Aristotelians argued
must inhabit the sublunar sphere
between the earth and moon
where change was permissible
those were the days in which theological arguments
were of passionate interest
we who live in a fragmented society
have become like an individual addicted
to psychoanalysis and pick at our virtues
and vices as if they were scabs
peat-water has a curious property
these leathery corpses are the distant ancestors
of the English-speaking peoples
the human animal and his emotions change
little from age to age
machines are ahead of morals
by some centuries
there must be hierarchy
Darwin assumed the electrons were free
when the collision occurred
but this led him to a radius
for the electronic orbit in the Rutherford model
that is far too large
he set others the task of creating small maps
in the Sintashta horse burials the legs
are arranged to imitate running
not one of them moved as I went by
but I felt the impact of dozens of black eyes
following me the white veils
falling across their backs
on the south side of the churchyard
is a tramline embedded
in the grass flung here on 11 April 1941

when a high-explosive bomb fell nearby
why else had the children of Israel
slept in graves if not
to be resurrected as more than others?
every mother is anxious
to pass on to her children
the gift of good looks
not Khaled only but every Moslem warrior
felt himself indeed to be the Sword of God
the country was cultivated for pleasure
as well as for need
everywhere the useful was attractive
the one enduring mark of Islam's origins
the adoption of the Arabic language
in the conquered lands
had early man's prime intention
been to design an astronomical instrument
it is unlikely he would have
constructed a circle
there was no reason to create subdivisions
for religions or ethnicity
early in the ninth century
a member of the House of Wisdom
compiled prayer-tables for the latitude of Baghdad
dissection of dead humans possibly
even experimenting on living slaves
first developed in Hellenistic Alexandria
experts in anatomy believe early hominids
may have evolved for climbing vertical
tree trunks grasping branches and feeding
with the arms and hands
a more generalised adaptation
than acrobatic arm-swinging
the attainer of immortality ascends
to heaven visibly or else seems
to die and be buried but when the coffin
is opened it is found to be empty

when Lenin seized power in 1917
he applied the German war model
to the task of making Russia
a great industrial power
the war had taught Mussolini
that nation is stronger than class
a thousand corpses lying in rain and sun
who but an English aristocrat
would turn Don Juan into a tourist?
a nobleman might read a book and acquire
some learning but surely not write one
the ordinary soldier make himself understood
only with motions and sundry gruntings
my hypothesis is that the kinetic energy
of an electron in orbit around the core
is related to its frequency of rotation
the usual modern translation
of civitates in the context of Britain
as tribes says more about recent views
than about the Romans' ideas
according to the chief of the OKW
the bombardment of Warsaw
and the shooting of the categories
of people mentioned before
had been agreed upon already
only a small quantity of electricity
is used by each lamp
the rock itself being used as a membrane
between two realms of existence
using all the biochemical techniques now available
and surveying as many proteins as possible
the overall genetic differences are remarkably small
Schönberg and Hildegard conferring at Ulm
ponder the numerical properties of a created music
the unfeasible height of the pelican in her piety
atop the carved wooden cover
on the font at Ufford in Suffolk

rivalled only at Nuremberg
we must undoubtedly criticise
wrong ideas of every description
banned as degenerate art
do not presume that wooden heads
are cut out with a knife
I could see them lying
on the sacking floor of the drying-room
clinging together with an intensity like fear
religion is not out of bounds to science
in spite of propaganda to the contrary
by aligning these arrangements
of stones and timbers on the moon
the sun and the stars chiefs or priests
could link their own power
to the rhythms and cycles of the world
comparing what they now were
with what they had been
in the times of their ignorance
when they worshipped
dead idols they felt they had learned
the true glory and dignity of man
wood carved cunningly to imitate
the spires and reticulated arches of stone
and to rise on its pulley in three telescopic sections
initially Taoism was concerned
with literal and physical immortality
which involved the quest for substances
and exercises which might produce this
the body is pregnant with symbolic meanings
often highly contradictory
the fisherman having finished his prayer
casts his nets a fourth time
sometimes running a lazy eye over
a text of which he already knows every word
he finds himself visualising the scene it evokes
shapes and sizes of tombs

vary a great deal from place to place
and from one period to another
in the climate of west Africa books rot
pianos go out of tune and
even gramophone records buckle
the aim is to read what was never written
such reading is the most ancient
on some days there is no variation at all
on others the line begins to veer a great deal
across the page creating peaks and troughs
I have had one or two moments
like that in my life

Ark of Marvels

A portrait of Julius Caesar, a looking-glass,
an African charm entirely made of teeth,
a north American canoe & a stone axe,
Napoleon's silver-handled toothbrush, a sign
from a Viennese apothecary's shop,
the bell & bauble of King Henry's fool,
a Dutch still-life, a bust of Attila the Hun,
a madonna fashioned in feathers from Indian birds,
a genealogical table of England's kings,
a needlework map of Britain, a striking likeness
of Moses, an organ in mother-of-pearl, a clock
with a mighty Ethiop riding astride a rhino,
a sundial shaped like a monkey, a mermaid's hand,
the tail, but not the horn, of a unicorn,
a pair of Galapagos terns & a taxidermied booby,
the last known dodo, an array of shoes
in every global style, a cunning machine
for translating sounds to colours,
images to series of musical notes & tones,
a Chinese torture chair of lethal blades,
a fine-carved Aztec sacrificial knife,
prosthetic limbs in polished wood & leather,
a pile of amputation saws, a device
for preventing masturbation (nickel-plated),
a brass corset, a chastity-belt of iron,
the mummified corpse of a young Peruvian boy,
a feeding-bottle in the rough shape of a bird,
an ivory model of a pregnant woman (open),
a case of assorted implements for birth,
a glass syringe, a guillotine blade (used),
a snuffbox in the head of a horned ram,
a dentist's signboard strung with 100 teeth,
the moccasins worn by Florence Nightingale,
three tons of worthless metal, five of old photos,

two of wood boulders, Darwin's walking-stick,
a case of 50 glass eyes, a wooden leg,
a Sinhalese dancing-mask, steel safe doors,
many useless tools, some obsolete hoists,
three and a half tons of swords, two and a half of guns,
cannons, helmets & shields, 110 cases
of Greco-Roman artefacts, 85
of surgical instruments, 60 of pestles & mortars,
a hoard of gourds from Guatemala &
an urn containing the ashes of the collector.

Museum Piece

A Lady apparently in a position to know
declared the prick of Napoleon less impressive
than Wellington's, which she presumably knew from life,
not mummified and sold at auction by Christie's.
In the Museum of Erotica at St Petersburg,
housed in a former clinic of social disease,
lies grey in a jar the 12-inch pickled member
of Rasputin, which may well explain the power
he wielded over the last insane tsarina,
thereby keeping the autocrat in thrall.
A relic unhappily lost is the foreskin of Christ,
once held to be holy by sad infertile women,
who flocked to kiss the vessel in which it lay.
Napoleon brushed his teeth with opium paste.

If You Live Long Enough You See Everything

the curlicues repeat indefinitely swirled
in self-similar writhing, a Mandelbrot set
of recursive fern, cauliflower and subatomic planets
by the wheeltapper's mallet and lamplighter's rod
the photographs, posters, stamps and licences
a lamp attached to a box for storing *yang yao*
pipes of ebony, ivory, bone, silver, iron
buffalo and rhinoceros horn, porcelain, jade
amber, tortoiseshell, enamelled glass or bamboo
simple pipes in special buildings
straight, curved, carved or ornately adorned
with lions, dragons and apes, a living Chinaman
displayed at Earls Court, where smoke behaves
differently, butterfly tattoos on the server's fingers
holding the beautiful with glasses and a pill
willow pattern staining on the exhalations
of a trumpeter at the reticulated gate

Halifax Road

Lunchtime May 27th

by Hilary Rainbow, 1941

"Well, we've sunk the Bismarck!"
"Oh good!" – spoon poised over the bright dish covers
(A light moment in our desultory conversations
Of food values & the increasing difficulties of the rations:
"Is there really enough protein content in a vegetable pie?)
Tooth for tooth & eye for eye –
"It was bad luck about the Hood
But now we're squared, so that's good."
And the disaster will soon vanish
Into the accounted-for and the to-be-expected
Chance issues by which our confidence is not affected,
Like the air-raids (unspeakable when they were Spanish),
But quick as grief I thought of you
And the unlived future smouldering in your eyes,
Trembling to new life and substance of dreams you knew
A deeper channel for earth's strength & the sea's & the sky's
Intended for God to use.
There is so much you have not tried,
You, and the others who are today's news.
"It's by an unlucky chance that they have died."
Maybe I haven't a grasp of the situation
And can't intelligently discuss the affairs of the nation,
I only know the chill in my marrow
And the cold grating of unspecified sorrow.

Domes of Silence

Still wearing the supplied gloves
I work the liquid carefully into the corners
as instructed,
remembering or imagining
all the places we might
have observed this effective ritual;
steps and towers by the river,
smoke curling round cupolas
in shaded glades.

You are not here now but still
the crows and the pariah kites
call and cry,
circling around the legs of the table
as I sit and quietly type.

Halifax Road

The house I was born in still stands,
between the moortop and the village rec –

the open moor where curlews call,
the swings where my sisters took me to play,

the patch of rough garden where my brother
sank a pit for a wooden moon-rocket.

The house I was born in was built with his own hands
by a weaver newly returned from the war

against Napoleon and revolutionary France
so he could settle and marry his sweetheart;

the couple who sold the house to my parents
remembered as children knowing that old man.

The house I was born in still looks out
over the valley, no longer smoky,

but still twinkling at night with the lights
of the old mill town

where the weaver's cloth was traded,
and the bus from the village ran.

Stand today by the once lonely house
and only when the wind howls loudest

will you lose the background sound
of tyres on tarmac and engines' growl

from the fuming traffic in people and freight
moving along that scratch on the map

scrawled between cities whose nighttime glow
looms and glowers over the open moor.

Phyllis

I am holding a teacup
   it rattles in the saucer
  I stand in a doorway
    rattling in the saucer
     I put the teacup on the mantelpiece
      I place the cup on the windowsill
    a district nurse comes in
     speaking words
   I do not understand
  I hold the teacup
rattling in the saucer
  I place it on the windowsill
   that is on the mantelpiece
    someone is looking on
   I think it is a district nurse
I am speaking words
  I do not understand
I am holding a teacup
  rattling in its saucer
   as I stand in the doorway
   maybe I am smiling
    as carefully I put the teacup
     on the windowsill
    the saucer is on the mantelpiece
   a district nurse is staring
at the cup on the mantelpiece
on the windowsill
 she is speaking a language
rattling in the saucer
  there is a grandmother in the doorway
   she is holding a teacup
    which rattles in the saucer
     carefully I place the teacup
      in the saucer on the windowsill

it does not rattle
I am standing with a teacup
balanced upon a saucer
I balance on a saucer in the doorway
place it upon the mantelpiece
there is tea spilled in the saucer
cold tea rattling in the cup
I put on the windowsill
speaking a language
I do not understand
there is a grandmother
rattling in the doorway
and speaking in language
on the mantelpiece
I am holding a teacup
it rattles in the saucer
I stand in a doorway
speaking like a district nurse
I will place carefully
on the windowsill
smiling in a language
I do not understand
as if a grandmother in the doorway
I know I am an aunt
not a grandmother or a nurse
I am almost sure I am smiling
I have not spilled tea in the rattling saucer
I am smiling at the teacup
I have placed carefully
on the mantelpiece
outside the window

Palimpsest III

I am wearing the wrong shoes. These
were undoubtedly never my father's.
The wolves will be offended,

the news unconscionable. We will be folded
and submerged, coming home late
baffled by astrological predictions.

It's weird, dear, almost verbally at the beginning,
how terrible was his face, wearing clothes
around the garden so innocently,

interested in torn-up history, and walking
towards a war that insists
on its own righteousness.

The talks are locked in stalemate,
a bishop maintaining silence
while pawns threaten your queen.

How eager some of us are
to dominate the laughing dead,
this softness in calm barrels. Silent war

reduces its prison and cools the ice.
We were made in the blood cluster
bars of the prayerbook and then

falling asleep to support the sharp sword
of afternoon near the poles, a map found
in a charity store, talking in more than one voice.

This voice reveals the curfew intelligence of a clock.
Break open the book – there is no electricity,
no lunchbreaks. There should be fresh polish,

hot water and other single dreams.
But it is only a voice that stands out
while talking to us: thy crime maps will be done.

Three Vignettes for Tom Raworth

Perspective

the joke
about writing's
in the words
he said

to see it
you have
to keep
an eye
the blind one
open

Ifs & Butts

barely furnished
in the little room
he employs
for ashtray
the lower drawer
of a desk
topped only
with a Remington
portable
bearing
a single blank sheet

I've run out
he says
meaning
paper
or coffee

or words
not cigarettes

proffering
the pack
he puts one
to his lips
lights
the wrong end
it smells foul
I keep
doing that
he says

At King's

something in the way she moves
attracts our gaze
from across the quad
or maybe it's the light
glinting on the chapel glass
I can't take pleasure
he says
in walking on the grass
when everyone's allowed to do it

Day Trip 1978

I eat an apple as if it was an ice-cream
and my ice-cream as if it were an apple
I am still here for now

coloured lighting bends
into the sky and back
reflected in the rain

advertising slogans
projected on the clouds
as voices quiver

between the buildings
rippling in the
water's surface

vision's affected
dreamlike refracting
images of fear

falling on sculpted
stonework and blades
of the lawn we lie on

the enclosing sky
and dim shadows
just out of sight

fear of returning to normalcy
where all will be changed
fear of not

puzzlement of how
a perceiver relates

to these perceptions

they will believe
I imagined I could fly
or intended self-annihilation

but it is only that the lawn
is so green and near
I could step out onto it

now dank hours must follow
and we subside
into our words

That Strange Geometry

after all these forty summers her face
now powder white
interrupts his nights

         her cold white face
                  bandied
         everywhere before him
         as he roams his little world
         swinging
                  between crutches

some storeys up, she descends into hell
– or is it escape? –
via the beckoning frame of a window

here then is the story
every story there is
the door hinged
to open either way

         she is no ghost
         for time is not present
         or past
              but is

yes, a window, geometric aperture
through which a woman – anyone –
may make an exit

         restlessly
              he moves
         among the arcane structures
         the complexity
                  set out by men

but was it the window
he saw her face
reflected in
or staring blankly through?

the windows polished and shone
the windows broken
shattered in the streets
leaving mannequins and their owners
exposed, still, barefaced, blank

the trap does not spring shut
but closes slowly
                irrevocably
impermeable

            where one's head is arranged
            at another's foot
            he, wandering, must
            seem a malignant growth
                            yet
            with his callipers he goes
            among and between
                          quartering
            the planet

she leaves behind her
a kerfuffle of papers
as she takes her last exit
through the high casement

            swerving in continuum
                        void
            beyond and above
                    such a sphere
            is merely veering
                    amid nothing

                    continuously: or time
                    is only distance
                                        movement

light from the window behind him
caught in his glasses
makes bright points on the paper

                    stoppage or continuation
                    departing or arrival
                    he
                        lusts
                    for climactic death; night
                    strangely holds him
                    but always
                                        the earth turns anew
                    to the sunrise
                                        and his numinous
                    visions are sent back
                                        diseased
to wherever they came from

she contemplates again the imperfection
in the glass
                that bubble
where clouds wiggle

                    should he select
                                        a door
                    or wait for one
                                        to swing
                    open in his direction?

seen from the bed, the window
is the scene of all life
all activity

of birds and neighbours
trades folk and the curious unknown

the strangest door
is the one
that closes silently behind him
leaving him
surprised
to find that all seems still
the same about him

the same

and not the same

Saddleworth

The moortop is burning,
smoke in the wind
a hazard for drivers.
Under the surface the earth
smoulders constantly, naked
flame seldom reaching the air
as now, in February – February
with a slight haze, yellowish
like pollen days, a gentle
stinging in the eyes. A pyre
for Keith, so long lost
now unrecoverable, bones
incorporated in the ashy soil.
Over poached eggs and crosswords
on Halifax Road
they talk of the coming summer
and keep the windows closed.

Forbidden Morning

Words from my mother's last weeks

I

for days after day
from Wednesday through afferloonish
I cline the meckavercally
swiffle and wishy cline and cline

feathermost blufle-flarget
blastle fothergit to the high, high
and then
blern or burble
cly and cly to
did it and got
gliffle the blufle-furger
and I so proun of yourself
as you may imagine

alvin to the felginstagle
trine and trine
cly and cly
cline in drene-tine
all in drene

days in Dayswater
blifflespurgen to the albenmeissen
droffle muster glingenmester
can you?

glorgle-musten
can you? can you?

I could sprifflemerstenhangenshunk
and so
to be honest with you
he glindle wandle handle bindle lendle
and so glindermandel metalfellickly
oh the rattle-poppenen, can you?

der meistersinger and some tessellin
smurgle-heissichneit
but may and may not
keep clining in drene
can you?
get you?
can you?
oh smelly spelly
some balderridge flashipus, yes?

II

bad tongue collapses klimmer-klammer till November
just wait till your father gets hope
she'll want to tessel the grave vondiheap
till the cowcomes
as courting of parrents tellifies
language dommage jessifies in brain
as well you know

III

I am too old
tomorrow

I might be gone

I may
tomorrow

how is it possible
for a person to forget
their dearest names?

it should be time
for finish

I feel
I often feel

if someone
would be so kind